1

Adam and his wife hid themselves from the presence of the Lord God

Genesis 3 v 8

God made man on the sixth day of creation and called him Adam. He was given a wife called Eve. They were told to take care of the earth and all the animals on it. They lived in a paradise called the Garden of Eden, and enjoyed being with God. There was a tree in the garden that they were told they could not eat from but the serpent tempted them and they ate. They knew they had disobeyed God and when he came into the garden they were frightened and hid from him.

Cain rose up against Abel his brother

Genesis 4 v 8

Adam and Eve were banished from the Garden of Eden for their disobedience and had to live off what they could grow in the ground. Eve's two eldest children were called Cain and Abel. When they grew up Cain looked after the crops and Abel kept the sheep. One day they brought gifts to God. The Lord was pleased with Abel's gift but not with Cain's. This made Cain so angry and jealous that he killed his brother.

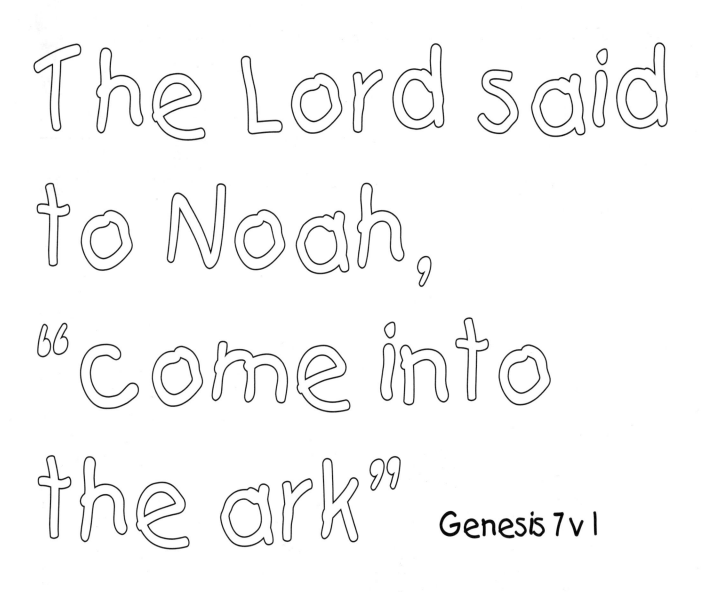

The Lord said to Noah, "come into the ark"

Genesis 7 v 1

As the years passed by, the people on earth became even more sinful and wicked. Because of their terrible behaviour God decided to destroy all life on earth with a huge flood. Only Noah and his family loved the Lord so God told him to build an ark and take two of every kind of creature onto it, so that they might all be safe, and fill the world with life again when the flood went away.

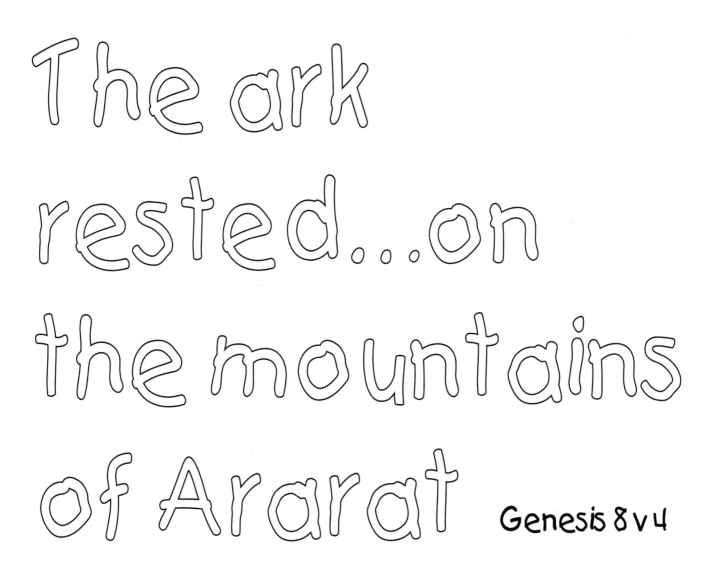

The ark rested...on the mountains of Ararat

Genesis 8 v 4

It rained for forty days and nights and the earth was flooded. All the animals and the wicked people were killed. When the rain stopped the water began to recede, and the ark came to rest on Mount Ararat. Noah, his family, and all the animals were quite safe.

Let us build ourselves...a tower whose top is in the heavens

Genesis 11 v 4

The earth was once again filled with many people from Noah's family. It did not take long for them to become as wicked as the earlier people and they decided that they were very powerful and would build a tower to reach to heaven. God stopped this from happening by making them speak in many different languages. They could not understand one another and so separated into groups who spoke the same language and were soon scattered all over the earth.

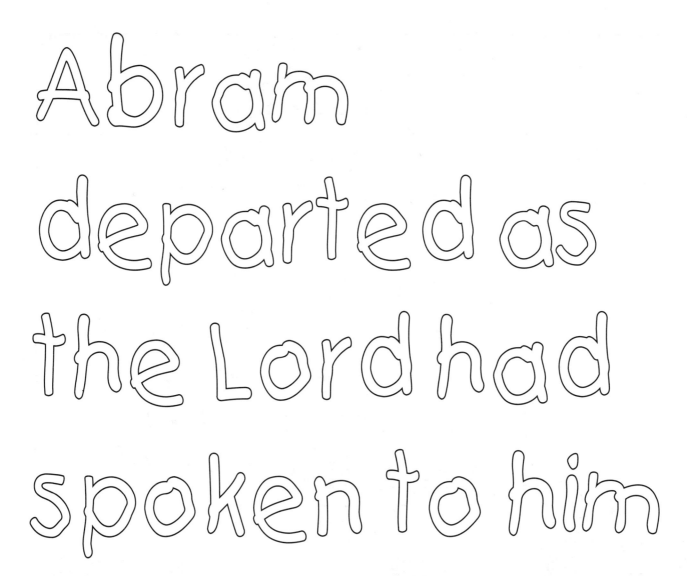

Abram departed as the Lord had spoken to him

Genesis 12 v 4

Abram was a good man, who loved God. He lived in a place called Haran, and his father, Terah, died there. God told Abram to go on a journey taking his family and servants. He would be led to another place. Abram's nephew, Lot, went too.

Get out of this place; for the Lord will destroy this city

Genesis 19 v 14

The servants of Abram and Lot argued so they separated and lived in different places. Lot lived near the wicked cities of Sodom and Gomorrah. God sent two messengers to warn him to leave the cities as they were going to be destroyed because the people living in them were so wicked. Lot, his wife and his two daughters obeyed and left. The cities were completely destroyed, as God had promised.

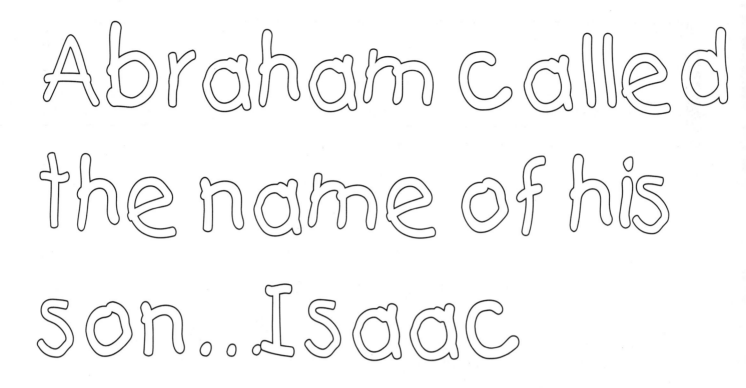

Abraham called the name of his son..Isaac

Genesis 21v 3

God changed Abram's name to Abraham, to show that he was the Lord's. He had promised him and his wife a child for many years but now they thought it was too late, because Abraham was 100 years old, and his wife, Sarah, was ninety years old. God fulfilled his promise, however, and Sarah had a son who was called Isaac.

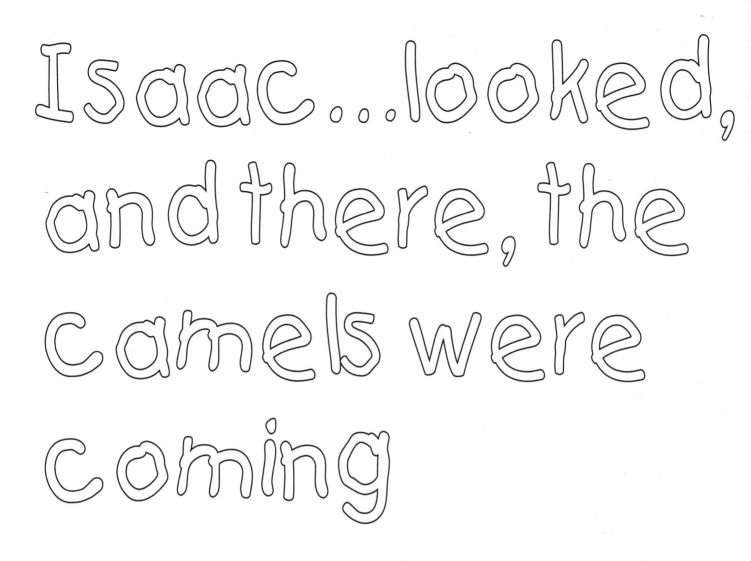

Isaac...looked, and there, the camels were coming

Genesis 24 v 63

After Sarah had died, Abraham told his oldest servant to return to his own country and bring back a wife for Isaac. God led Abraham's servant to a girl called Rebekah. As they all returned to Abraham's camp they saw Isaac walking towards them. Isaac and Rebekah loved one another and were married.

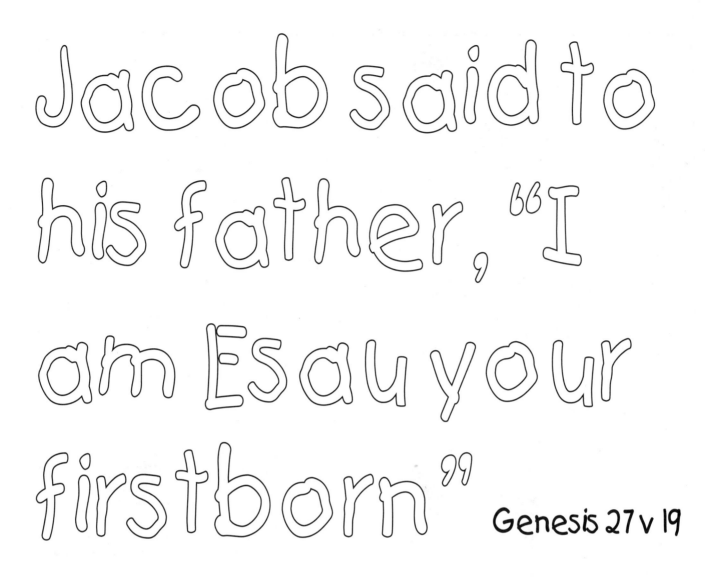

Jacob said to his father, "I am Esau your firstborn"

Genesis 27 v 19

Isaac and Rebekah had twin sons, called Esau and Jacob. Isaac loved the oldest, Esau more but Rebekah preferred Jacob, the youngest. As the eldest Esau should have received a blessing from Isaac but Jacob cheated his brother by dressing up and pretending to be him. Isaac was blind and was deceived and gave Jacob the blessing meant for Esau.

Rachel came with her father's sheep

Genesis 29 v 9

Esau was so angry that Jacob had to run away. Rebekah sent him to her brother's country. While travelling, Jacob vowed to accept the Lord as his one true God. He sat by a well because he was tired and a young girl gave him some water. He discovered that she was Rachel, his cousin.

Israel loved Joseph...he made him a tunic of many colours

Genesis 37 v 3

God changed Jacob's name to Israel. He had twelve sons, the two youngest being Rachel's. They were called Joseph and Benjamin. Joseph was Israel's favourite and he showed this by giving him a coat of many colours.

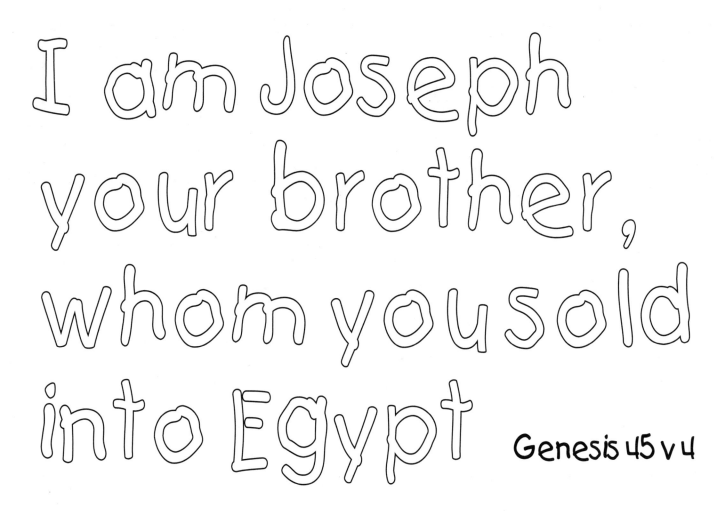

I am Joseph your brother, whom you sold into Egypt

Genesis 45 v 4

Joseph's brothers were very jealous and sold him into Egypt as a slave. Israel thought Joseph had been killed by a wild beast. God had a plan for Joseph in Egypt and he was kept safe, and reached a position of great authority. During a famine he was put in charge of all the food that had been gathered. His brothers came to Egypt to buy food and he told them who he was. All the family came to live in Egypt, which was God's plan.

THE STORY OF ABRAHAM. God promised that he would make Abram's name great, and bless all of his people. Abram left Haran, taking his wife Sarai, and his nephew, Lot, with him. Abram was seventy-five when he left, and they entered the land of Canaan.

Find out more in Book 4